Samuel Boyer Davis

Escape of a Confederate Officer From Prison

What he saw at Andersonville - how he was sentenced to death and saved by the interposition of President Abraham Lincoln

Samuel Boyer Davis

Escape of a Confederate Officer From Prison
What he saw at Andersonville - how he was sentenced to death and saved by the interposition of President Abraham Lincoln

ISBN/EAN: 9783337119911

Printed in Europe, USA, Canada, Australia, Japan

Cover: Foto ©ninafisch / pixelio.de

More available books at **www.hansebooks.com**

ESCAPE OF A CONFEDERATE OFFICER FROM PRISON.

WHAT HE SAW AT ANDERSONVILLE.

HOW HE WAS SENTENCED TO DEATH AND SAVED BY THE INTERPOSITION OF President Abraham Lincoln.

NORFOLK, VA.:
THE LANDMARK PUBLISHING COMPANY.
1892.

Entered according to Act of Congress, in the year 1892,

By SAMUEL B. DAVIS,

In the office of the Librarian of Congress,
at Washington.

THE CONFEDERATE SPY.

THROUGH THE UNION LINES AND MANY PERILS.

Daring Mission of a Young Confederate Officer to Ohio and to Canada—Narrow Escape from the Gallows.

WAS THIS ANOTHER ANDRE CASE?

The above was the heading of an article which recently appeared in at least one newspaper published in Virginia, and it began as follows:

"Lt. S. B. Davis, of the Confederate Service, probably came the nearest of any officer on either side to playing the role of the Andre of the Rebellion."

So it began, and the ending was:

"To the end he kept the secret of his mission to Ohio."

A letter written to the author of the above brought me the information that he had gotten his points "by following the account given by Capt. Hines, and a narrative before the Loyal Legion, by a member of the Court." The article referred to has caused my friends to ask why I have never written an account of what I went through during the War. In order to make a connected story, let me begin at the Battle of Gettysburg, where I was shot through the lung. Then my recollections of Andersonville, from the outside of the prison, and conclude with my trip to Canada.

A Recollection of the War.

At the Battle of Gettysburg I was Aid to Major Genl. Trimble, of Maryland. In the third day's fight, while with one of the divisions, supporting Pickett in his memorable charge, I was shot through the lung and taken prisoner by the United States forces, who advanced after the Confederates had fallen back. Two Portugese Soldiers were the first persons I saw after the skirmish line had passed over me, and I asked them for a little water to drink; they carried me up the hill and laid me down behind the stone wall I had so much wished to reach only a short time before, but under different circumstances.

A very diminutive surgeon of Teutonic persuasion came my way, and to satisfy myself I was not going to die, I asked him to examine my wound. He was kind, and said in his broken-English, "Yes, I look at dat vound," and he did so. I pressed him to tell me what he thought of it, but I could only draw from his doleful countenance and the ominous shaking of his head the most discouraging conclusions as to my chances of recovery. Determined to settle the matter, if possible, in order that I might let it be known to my friends that I had been killed, I pressed him still further, but without avail; all I could get him to say was: "It is very dangerous." Worried at my failure to get at his conviction, I tried once more, assuring him he could not do me any injury by telling me the truth, as I was not afraid to die; while any encouragement he could and would give me, might go far towards helping me to live, which I was very anxious to do. In this way I got him to unbend a little, and after again examining the wound, this is what he said:

> "I tell you vat I dink,
> "I dink the possibility is you get vell,
> "I dink the probability is you die,
> "I dink by God you die anyhow."

I accepted the possibilities, and let the probabilities pass on. He gave me some morphia, put me on a stretcher, and I saw him no more. On the way to the field hospital, one of the men carrying me was shot, and I was dropped out of the stretcher, but I reached the field hospital, an old barn, with no further mishap.

Next day I was removed to another hospital, and in a day or two was sent to Baltimore, thence to Chester Pennsylvania. The Hospital at Chester being an old college on the site where afterwards stood the Pennsylvania Military Academy. I soon commenced to recover, and by the 10th of August began to cast about me for a chance to escape. I was very familiar with the whole surrounding country, and was sure if I could only get outside the line of sentinels, I would soon be back within the Confederate lines. I was afraid, however, to approach any one on the subject, as I was assured by older heads than mine among the officers confined with me, that if I tried to escape I would most assuredly be caught, and be subjected to close confinement and short rations. I could not, however, divest myself of the idea that I could get out, and at last I found among my fellow prisioners Capt. Slay, 16th Mississippi Regiment, who told me that he had had an offer made to him by one of the sentinels; that the sentinel sympathized with us, and would let any one or two of us escape, if he (Slay) wanted to get out. The only thing he asked was five dollars with which to escape himself if necessary.

After much advice from some of the other officers confined there against our making the attempt, Capt. Slay and myself concluded that upon the old theory "Faint heart ne'er won fair lady" and that if we remained there we would soon be sent from hospital to prison, with the uncertainty of exchange ahead of us, so we made up our minds to brave all danger and try to escape. I had already obtained a suit of gray clothes, not cut like a uniform, and of a lighter color than that usually worn by the Confederates; I traded my cap for a slouch hat, and I was equipped. Accordingly, after several interviews with our friend, the Sentinel, it was arranged that at fifteen minutes past twelve o'clock, on the night of the 16th of August, 1863, Capt. Slay and myself were to present ourselves at the post of the "friendly sentry," and he was to give us the countersign, and let us pass out of the lines. This night had been selected, because on the morning following it was reported that three hundred privates were to be sent to City Point for exchange, and we wished to leave the impression that we had managed to secrete ourselves among them.

Of course we were much excited at the prospect ahead of us, and for several days before the 16th arrived, we thought over our route and weighed fully the pros and cons of the expedition. At last the sixteenth came. As night came on the sky clouded up, and from 9 till 11 o'clock it rained in torrents, accompanied by thunder and lightning. By twelve the storm had ceased, and as it was cloudy and dark, we hoped to get off safe. I was now apparently quite well, although only six weeks had passed since I had been shot. I had taken what exercise I could, and concluded I was able to go. Capt. Slay had been shot through the left fore-arm the same day I was shot, but his arm had gotten so he could use it, and we two crippled Confederates started for a tramp back to Richmond.

Two of our friends accompanied us down stairs, partially clad, in order not to excite suspicion, and then gave us the garments they had brought, which clothed us fully. We managed to get out of the building without attracting any one's attention, and approached the spot where we knew the sentinel we wanted would be posted, at a concerted signal we heard the click, click of the musket. I must admit I was very uneasy unless we should have made some mistake and fallen on the wrong man; however, we soon heard "Advance and give the countersign." We advanced—"Farewell, God bless you." He sang out "the countersign is right; pass on," and we were free. We did not lose any time, I assure you, in putting as much ground as we could between the hospital and ourselves, and daylight found us walking into Wilmington, Delaware. It was no easy work for two badly wounded men to walk fifteen miles so soon after being shot, and although we were much fatigued, we felt to the fullest extent the importance of still further effort on our part to continue our tramp. We knew, however, that the roll was never called at Chester until after 9 o'clock A. M., and being very hungry we determined to have some breakfast. Accordingly, we went to the United States Hotel, and had the pleasure (?) of enjoying our breakfast at the table with Brig.-Gen. Tyler, U. S. A. He was accompanied by his staff, all in uniform, and I leave you to imagine the feelings of two escaped "Johnnie Rebs" at breakfast with such company. The meal over, we hastened to get out of town as soon as possible.

Deeming it prudent to get away from the more frequented thoroughfares, and feeling sure that as soon as we were missed the authorities would wire to Baltimore, where I was known to have relatives and friends. I determined to strike down the Delaware Peninsula, and accordingly on leaving Wilmington behind us, we took the road to New Castle. When we had reached a point half way between Wilmington and New Castle, tired nature began to assert herself, and worn out by excitement and our long tramp, we were forced to seek rest in a piece of woods by the roadside. Up to this time (had we known as much then as I found out afterwards) we had not been reported as missing; and I may as well say here how I gained this information. At Chester there was in charge of the ward, where Slay and myself were placed, a hospital steward, whose name, if memory serves me well, was Riker, or something similar. A year after our escape, and when I was at Andersonville, this same man recognized me while I was riding through the stockade; although he could not overtake me, he followed me to the gate and asked the officer on duty there to send him to headquarters that he might see me. His request was granted, and I at once knew him and paroled him to duty in the office of which I had charge. He told me that Capt. Slay and myself were not missed for twenty-four hours after our departue, and that then Baltimore and Philadelphia were the only points where the authorities were notified to lookout for us; in the meantime we were tramping through Delaware. Riker also told me a piece of news I was very sorry to hear, and that was that our friend, the Sentinel, had unwisely let fall a clew by which he was accused and convicted of having let us out. I have never heard what became of either Riker or the Sentinel.

After several hours of needed rest, we again started on our journey, arrived at New Castle, we were obliged to wait two hours for a train to Dover. It being my intention to go from Dover over the line into Maryland, cross the Chesapeake Bay, and get to the Potomac river as soon as possible. Finally the train at 6 P. M. rolled up to the station, but much to our chagrin, on our entrance into a car we saw Col. Willis, of New Jersey, who had been until within the last week at Chester, and with whom both of us had frequently conversed. In addition to this there was also a corporal and three soldiers in the car.

Frightened as we were, we still had presence of mind enough to separate at once. I took a whole seat to myself, and curling up on the cushion in a manner to as fully as possible hide my face, feigned sleep. Slay fixed himself as best he could, and threw a handerchief over his face, and tried by heavy breathing to convince every one that he, too, was napping. As I lay there trembling with the fear of being apprehended, all the advice of those I had left behind rushed through my brain. Visions of these soldiers in the car coming after me crowded upon me in every conceivable shape; every time I heard some restless passenger or one of the train men walk through the car, I could almost feel the hand touch me and hear the irons close around my wrists. After several stations had been passed, I ventured to peep out, and I was to some extent relieved to find the colonel had left the train. In a little while more the train stopped at Smyrna, and to our joy and unspeakable relief the soldiers departed and again we felt assured. While we remained at Chester in the hospital, Capt. Slay had met among the visitors who came there, one or two ladies from Dover. These ladies had told him if he could escape and come to Dover they would do all they could to pass him on to Dixie. Accordingly on our arrival at Dover, he, against my judgment, insisted on calling on these ladies. I had two reasons for not wanting him to do so: first, I feared that he might meet some one there before whom he would be forced to, or would explain himself, and get us into trouble; second, I knew that the sentiment in Delaware was to some extent divided, and his going to see these ladies would, if found out, cause them much annoyance if not very serious trouble; so I declined to go with him. He went, however, alone, and after an hour I was delighted to see him return without having had any mishap. Having made arrangements for a very early start next morning, we laid down and slept soundly. A carriage was in waiting for us as soon as breakfast was over in the morning, and we started on a drive of 30 or 40 miles to Easton, Maryland. We had now gotten on to country roads, away from railroads, etc., and began to feel for the time safe. The weather was fair, and while we could not converse on the subject uppermost in our minds (less the driver find us out), we managed to pass the day in a fairly comfortable manner. At a place called Greenville, I think it is near the dividing line between Delaware and Maryland, we stopped for dinner and to feed and refresh our horses. I recall now how astonished both Capt. Slay and myself were at the time at the very moderate price charged us for three dinners, and horse feed, but we had been accustomed to paying Confederate prices for whatever we had, and the country prices of the Delaware peninsula were new to us. We reached Easton just at dusk, and after a hasty supper retired early as we considered it best to keep for the present, as much out of sight as possible. The next morning we dismissed our Dover equipage, and started for a tramp of 11 miles to a part of the country where I knew we would find friends. That night we slept at the house of a gentleman who has since held a place of some prominence under the State government. The next day after a drive of nine miles we took the good steamer "Kent" from Miles River Ferry, and again started for "Dixie." In boarding the steamer we were obliged to pass between United States soldiers on guard at the gangway. I did not at first understand this, but soon learned that there was a company of negro recruits on the steamer, and the guard was placed to prevent any desertions from their ranks. The proximity of United States troops very naturally threw a feeling of unrest over us, but they paid no attention to us, and we did not, I assure you, in any way disturb them.

In those days it was the custom for certain persons, patrons of the steamboat company, to row out from their farms and board the steamer in the stream. Shortly after leaving Miles River Ferry, the steamer stopped and there came on board from his farm Mr. Williams, of Baltimore. I had known him before I went south, but I had not seen him for several years, and I felt sure he would not recognize me. I took no pains, therefore, to keep clear of him, but stood boldly up by the side of the Provost in charge of the troops, looking on, as Mr. Williams came out in his boat. He came on board and walked right up to me and said, extending his hand, "Why, how are you, Davis; I thought you were in the Southern Army." All around us heard him; all eyes centered on me. Slay picked up the steamer's Bible and began to read, and I— well I was simply paralyzed with fright. I looked him full in the face, however, and said, "You are mistaken, sir; my name is Dawson." He apologized, saying I looked very much like his friend Davis, but that he felt sure he was down South. He passed on; I made some remark to the Provost and took a seat by Slay, much relieved. Years afterwards, on one occasion, I met Mr. Williams at a dinner in Baltimore, and he told me then he was sure he was right, and that he had spoken to the right man, but if he had been a detective on watch for me and known I was in that neighborhood, the coolness with which I answered him would have decived him.

West River Landing was soon reached, and we started full tilt for the Potomac. It was about 60 miles to the river, and both of us were feeling nearly played out. More than once we had thought that we had started from Chester in too enfeebled a condition, but there was no help now, and we must go ahead. Our course lay through a country where I knew we would be kindly received by most of the people, but I feared to go to a house lest there might be some who would not be glad to see us, so we trudged on without looking to right or left, until late into the night, when we laid down in the woods to rest. We were both so tired that when we waked the sun was shining brightly, and we hurried on. After a little while we met in the road an old gentleman on horseback, who seemed anxious to talk. At first we were shy of him, but before long we found he was in sympathy with the South and we told him who we were, and asked him to tell us where to get something to eat. He took us home, and after plenty to eat and drink we shook hands with our old friend and departed on our way rejoicing. The next morning brought us to a place called Allen's Fresh, Charles county, Md. After spending a day and two nights here, trying to get a boat to cross the Potomac in, and having at last succeeded, we went to Chapel Point, on Port Tobacco bay. It is here that the old Catholic Church, "St. Thomas," is situated, and it is one of the oldest churches in this country.

Having bought the boat, it was decided to wait

till the person from whom we obtained it, should be able to tell us that the river was clear of gunboats, and transports; this detained us for two nights longer. On the third night at 9 o'clock, we started to row across the river, which, including the bay, was about five miles; but we were doomed to disappointment. We lost our way, and after pulling about for several hours, we returned to where we started from, much to our disgust, and to the chagrin of the boatman. The next night we had better luck and about 12 o'clock we reached the Virginia shore, at Mathias Point; scrambling up the river bank, we set off for Port Conway, 12 miles distant, on the Rappahannock river. After a tramp of 10 miles and when we began to hope all was safe, a noise attracted our attention, and looking up we saw a soldier, gun and all, ahead of us, and the worst of it was he saw us. Too late to retreat, we had to approach him, and we did so with varied feelings of hope and fear. The fellow had on a pair of blue United States trousers, but a soft felt hat, and it was a question whether we had fallen on a Yankee, or a Johnnie. We soon found, however, that that "Yank" belonged to an Alabama regiment, and we were safe. The next day we took train for Richmond, and on the following morning this is what the papers said:

"One by one our prisoners in the North continue to make their escape from the torture and thraldom of the Yankee prisons. Among those who have recently escaped and made their way to the South, are Captains Davis and Slay, who arrived safely here last evening. They were both wounded and taken prisoners at the Battle of Gettysburg; they were first taken to Baltimore, thence to Chester, Pennsylvania, where they remained up to two weeks ago; making their escape and wending their way through the States of Pennsylvania, Delaware,

A RECOLLECTION OF THE WAR. 15

and Maryland, they succeeded in landing safely on the Virginia shore. On the way they met with many friends who kindly assisted them to all they wanted. They were 13 days on the way, braving hunger, fatigue and exposure. Both gentlemen belong to Major-Gen. Trimball's Division; Capt. Davis being one of his aids, and was shot through the right lung; Capt. Slay belongs to one of the Mississippi regiments, and was shot in the left arm. They left behind them at Chester 1,500 Confederates.

The day after we arrived in Richmond, Slay and myself separated to visit our different friends. Once only did I afterwards see him. He, like myself, was prostrated by the exertion, and both of us were for a long time laid up with typhoid fever. Both recovered, and in the late fall of '63 I saw Slay for the last time. When the spring campaign opened he returned to his regiment and the poor fellow was killed in the Battle of the Wilderness.

Late in October, 1863, I reported for duty, and was assigned to Genl. Jno. H. Winder as A. A. I. G. and remained in Richmond until the following spring. I left Richmond on the 27th of May, 1864, and after a brief stay at Goldsboro, N. C., (to which place Genl. Winder had been assigned to duty,) I was ordered on the 9th of June to proceed to Andersonville, Ga. I arrived there June 20th, and although I had left Genl. Winder at Goldsboro, I found on my arrival that he had reached Andersonville three days before me, namely, 17th June, 1864, and although I have seen it stated that he took charge there in the previous April, I know that his first appearance at Andersonville was as above stated. At the time that I arrived the stockade was being enlarged. It had originally been an enclosure of 18 acres, and intended to accommodate from six to ten thousand men, but the rapidly increasing number of prisoners caused the necessity of enlarging the enclosure, and an additional 10 acres was added, making 28 acres in all. The mode of building the stockade was as follows :

A trench four feet deep and two feet wide was dug, and after large pine trees had been hewn square they were set up in the trench as close together as possible, four feet in the ground and 20 feet above ground, the upper end being sharpened to a point. There was only one row of fence, inside of which and 20 feet therefrom, was the "dead line" which was a line of posts about four feet high with a plank four inches wide, nailed from post to post. This was all the enclosure called "The Stockade" at Andersonville.

I had been at Andersonville only four days when Gen. Winder sent me back to Richmond with letters to Gen. Sam'l Cooper, Adjt. Gen., urging the necessity of more prison room, and also dwelling on the importance that no more prisoners should be sent to Andersonville for two reasons: first, they were already over-crowded, and it was even then with much difficulty that provisions could be had to feed them, and any further addition to their number would increase this difficulty; second, he urged the fact that the risk of keeping so large a number of prisoners at one place was exceedingly dangerous, when it was considered that they were guarded only by old men and boys, the former over 60 years of age, the latter less than 18, and again that there were a very few, even of these, so few indeed that it rendered the force entirely inadequate for the duty required of them. In order to verify my recollections about the above referred to letter, I wrote to Capt. W. S. Winder, in whose possession is the *original order book used at Andersonville*, and asked him to send me a copy of the order sending me to Richmond, and also a copy of the letter I took to the Adjutant General. I am, therefore, through his kindness, enabled to give the order and the full text of the letter. Capt. Winder writes as follows :

Mr. S. B. Davis,

At your request I give below copy of the order sending you to Richmond from Andersonville and also a copy of the letter which you took to Gen. Cooper, Adjt. and Inspector Gen.
Yours truly,
W. S. WINDER.

Headquarters Post Camp Sumpter. }
Andersonville, Ga., June 24th, 1864. }

Special Order No. 110.
 I. * * * * * * *
 II. Lieut. S. Boyer Davis, A. A. I. G., will proceed at once to Richmond, Virginia, and report to the Adjt. and Inspector Gen. with certain important documents and papers, and return to this post as soon as he has accomplished his purpose.
 III. * * * * * * *
 IV. * * * * * * *
By order of Brig.-Gen. J. H. WINDER,
W. S. WINDER,
A. A. G.

Camp Sumpter, }
Andersonville, Georgia, }
June 24th, 1864. }

General—

The pressing necessity of the post and the great irregularity of the mails, have induced me to send Lieutenant Davis with this letter, though I can very illy spare his services as he is one of my most efficient assistants.

The state of affairs at this post is in a critical condition.

We have here largely over 24,000 prisioners of war and 1205 very raw troops—Georgia Reserves, with the measels prevailing, badly armed and worse disciplined to guard them. The prisoners rendered more desperate from the necessarily uncomfortable condition in which they are placed.

With the present force, a raid on the post would almost of necessity be successful, as the prisoners would occupy the attention of the troops. I do most conscientiously think the force should be largely reinforced, and I respectfully ask that it be done with the least possible delay

There has been and I am satisfied that there is now going on, a correspondence in the prison, with disaffected persons outside and I have every reason to believe that just before my arrival an agent of Gen. Sherman had been here tampering with the prisoners. From the information I have been able to collect since I have been here, I am satisfied that there is a portion of the population around here who ought to be looked after, and who actively sympathize with the prisoners. In order to enable me to watch and counteract this influence, I respectfully ask that Capt. D. W. Vowles, with a detailed man by the name of Weatherford, on the police at Richmond, and two other well selected detectives, be ordered to Report to me immediately.

It is difficult for those at a distance to realize the great responsibility of the command of this post, and the great danger of a successful outbreak among the prisoners; 25,000 men by the mere force of numbers can accomplish a great deal. If successful, the result would be much more disastrous than a defeat of the armies. It would result in the total ruin and devastation of this whole section of country; every house would be burned, violence to the women, destruction of crops, carrying off negroes, horses, mules and wagons. It is almost impossible to estimate the extent of such a disaster; a little timely, prudent preparation will render it impossible.

The rawness of the troops, the almost impossibility of getting a court-martial from the " Department of South Carolina and Georgia," and other circumstances connected with the prisoners, renders it very necessary that I should have the power to order court-martials, and I respectfully request that such an arrangement be made.

Let me again press upon the attention of the Department the great danger hanging over this post, and to the necessary steps to avert it. *Another prison should be immediately established as recommended in my former letter, and that no more prisoners be sent to this post.* The force is becoming too ponderous, and, indeed, it is not possible with my present means to extend the post fast enough to meet the demands; within the last four days we have discovered two extensive tunnels reaching outside the stockade, showing great industry and determination on the part of the prisoners. I am, very respectfully,

Your obedient servant,
JOHN H. WINDER,
Brig.-Gen.

To Gen. S. COOPER,
Adjt. and In.-Gen., Richmond, Va.

P. S.—We have just discovered a tunnel reaching 130 feet outside the stockade.

My trip to Richmond was an uneventful one, save of such trouble as can be rightly looked for on such a journey and in time of war. The Petersburg and Weldon railroad had been cut by the Federals, and I was obliged to run the gauntlet of both armies on a hand car. Once a party of Confederate Cavalry rushed in on several of us, and we came very near being shot by them. I reached Richmond in safety and delivered my letter, and next morning was sent to see President Jefferson Davis, that he might question me personally in regard to all matters connected with Andersonville. On my arrival back at Andersonville on the 18th of July, I found that in compliance with telegraphic and written instructions which had preceded me, Major Griswold had been sent to Alabama, and Captains Vowles and W. S. Winder to other localities to select and build other prisons as rapidly as possible. All this could not be done as rapidly as the emergency demanded, and the prisoners continued to crowd in on Andersonville, simply because there was nowhere else to send them, and to this fact may be laid a part of the suffering at Andersonville.

Owing to there being nowhere else to send them, and on account of the refusal of the Federal Government to exchange Federal prisoners, the following order had been issued :

Adjt. Inspector-Gen. Office,
Richmond, Va., May 2d, 1864.

General Order No. 45.

I. Prisoners captured south of Richmond will be sent direct to Andersonville, Sumpter county, Georgia.

(Signed) SAMUEL COOPER,
A. and In.-Gen.

On the 21st July, 1864, I was ordered to take charge of the prison at Macon, where there were 1,200 officers confined. I was in charge there about two weeks. I do not think there was any more complaint among the prisoners at Macon than there is likely to be among a crowd of men confined and not allowed to do as they please; but it was not a nice place to spend the summer, and there were innumerable efforts, and, I am sure, some successful attempts made to escape. I recollect once being at the gate when a cart doing some hauling was on its way out of the prison; behind came a man black as the ace of spades, with a shovel over his shoulders, pretending to be a laborer, but I saw the poor fellow was a soldier and had him stopped and locked up until some of his comrades could furnish him with a pair of blue trousers, when he was returned to the prison and his friends.

After I had been at Macon a short time, some of the officers who were paroled came to me and said that they had heard that a friend of theirs (a colonel), who was with stoneman in his raid, and who had been mortally wounded, was in a hospital in Macon, and was very anxious to see one or two of the officers confined in the prison, in order to send his last messages to his wife and family. Upon inquiry, I found the case to be a *bona fide* one, and I sent the prison Adjutant with the two officers to to visit the wounded colonel. The officers were under parole, and I sent no guard, save the adjutant; he to act more as a guide and as protection than anything else. They returned in an hour. The next morning I was relieved by the Colonel commanding the post and returned to Andersonville.

On my arrival there I asked for a court-martial, but after hearing from the officer commanding at Macon, Gen. Winder refused to call a trial, and he said I had only done what any kind and humane man would have done under the circumstances. My only object in reciting the above incident is to show that Gen. Winder was not the harsh and cruel man that some persons have seen fit to describe him, but that this was one instance at least when he commended an officer for kindness to a prisoner.

The next day, after the above matter was settled, I was ordered to assist Capt. Wirz, in charge of the prison at Anersonville. This was brought about by Wirz being quite sick. I had only been on duty as above stated for a day or two, when he (Wirz) was taken seriously ill, and I was put in charge in his place.

As near as I can get at the dates from some old papers I have, I think it was on the 13th or 14th of August that I relieved Capt. Wirz.

It may be well, before telling what I saw both inside and outside the prison, to look at the selection of the place, why it was selected, and how and what was done before prisoners were sent there.

There appeared in the *New York Day Book*, under date of October 14, 1865, and also (on account of demand for copies of that edition) on January 13, 1866, an article which tells so much truth about the selection of Andersonville, the difficulties surrounding its completion, and other things connected therewith, that I may be pardoned for making many extracts from it.

"The Federal pressure around Richmond, which rendered the receipt of supplies precarious, and the raids invited in hopes of releasing prisoners there, rendered the presence of so many prisoners a serious incumbrance."

It was determined to remove those then there, to the extent of 6000, to some place south where there would be the least danger from raids, and less transportation necessary of supplies for the prisoners. An officer was appointed with instructions to select a site on the Southwestern railroad, having reference to the following points: "A healthy locality, plenty of pure, good water, a running stream, and if possible shade trees, and in immediate neighborhood of grist and saw mills."

I am able to insert here a copy of the original order to Capt. Winder to select site for prison.

Headquarters Department of Henrico,
Richmond, November 24th, 1863.

Captain—

The Secretary of War directs that a prison for Federal Prisoners shall be established in the State of Georgia. The General commanding the department directs that you proceed without delay to select a site for that purpose in the neighborhood of Americus or Fort Valley, a town between Macon and Andersonville.

You will go by way of Milledgeville to consult Gov. Brown; and also by way of Atlanta to consult Gen. Cobb.

You will hold yourself in readiness to return to these Headquarters as soon as ordered.

Very respectfully,
Your obedient servant,
J. M. PEGRAM,
Capt. W. S. WINDER,   A. A. Gen.
A. A. Gen.

Capt. Winder did call upon Gov. Brown, at Milledgeville, and the legislature being in session the Governor introduced him to many of the members from southwestern Georgia, with the request that they would assist him by any suggestions they might have to make.

From the Governor and members of the legislature he received letters of introduction to many prominent men of Americus and Albany. After leaving Milledgeville, Capt. Winder went to Atlanta to consult Gen. Howell Cobb, then in command of that department, and received from him letters to several prominent citizens,

Could it be possible to have given instructions more explicit, or more in accordance with the desire to care for the comforts of the unfortunate men to be confined there. Did I say "comforts?" Of these there were none; nor have I seen any comfort in any prison, and I have been accorded the opportunity of judging from the outside, in the South, as well as on the inside; at Johnson's Island, Fort Delaware, Military Prison at Albany and Fort Warren, as well as various smaller prisons where I was temporarily kept. I wish, however, to show that the persons who ordered the selection of Andersonville, the person who selected it and the officer in command there, were influenced by the humane wish to do all they could for the men whom the Federal Government forced to be confined there, and I call attention in the first place to the above given extract, viz:

"A healthy locality, plenty of pure water, a running stream, and if possible shade trees, and in immediate neighborhood of grist and saw mills," and I say truly that these requirements were fulfilled as far as could be, except in the one fact that there were no shade trees. If it be asked why there were no shade trees, I answer: all through the pine tree country and in the light sandy soil that produce the tall Georgia pine, you will find that whenever a house is to be built that the first move is to cut down all pine trees within reach of the house; that is all trees which by falling could fall on or in the immediate vicinity of the house. It is well-known that the roots of tall pines have an insufficient hold on the light soil that produces them, and hence the necessity to remove the tree. The trees at Andersonville were cut down for this reason—all the trees that were in the enclosure were pine. Like the writer of the article referred to I never have heard the healthiness of the locality questioned, and to still further show that this was one point made necessary in the selection of a prison site. One writer, named Spencer, in his bitter comments on Andersonville and those connected therewith, admits in his book that an officer was sent to visit various places in search of a suitable and healthy site. Among others, one in the town of Albany, Dougherty county, Ga. "It is supposed, however," says the writer, "that the opposition of those holding interest near the place, coupled with arguments of its unhealthfulness was sufficient to prevent its selection."

As to the water, there was running through the stockade, at Andersonville, a stream at least 20 or 25 feet wide; it had its origin in two large springs half a mile above the prison; immediately before entering the prison, the two streams issuing from these springs formed a junction, and the stream thus formed ran through the prison; it never went dry; it had a constant flow, and always one way. That portion of the stream within the prison was divided into three parts. The first, where it entered the stockade, was used as drinking water; in the center of the enclosure for bathing purposes; but, alas, I fear this part was seldom, if ever, used, while near its exit from the place was used for sinks, etc. I am very well aware that great stress has been laid on the water question; that the water was polluted before it reached the prison by persons in the cook house just outside; this cookery was run by paroled prisoners, and if the water was defiled in any way it was done by them; is it likely they would do so knowing their comrades had it to drink? The guards who were stationed at the gate drank of the same water; could it have been hurt by simply passing under the fence? Besides this stream, there were many wells in the stockade; some were dug by the prisoners themselves and some by the Confederate authorities. But I have known prisoners to dig and claim a well and refuse to give a drink of water therefrom to one of their suffering comrades unless he paid for it.

"In regard to the sufferings and mortality among the prisoners at Andersonville, none of it arose from the unhealthiness of the locality. The food, though the same as that used by the Confederate soldiers, the bread, too, being corn, was different from that to which they had been accustomed, did not agree with them, and scurvy and diarrhœa prevailed to a considerable extent. Neither disease, however, is the result of starvation."—*New York Day Book*, Jan. 13, 1866.

That some of the prisoners confined at Andersonville did not get their full allowance, I doubt not is true; but whose fault was it? During the time that I was there, the latter part of August, 1864, there were in operation outside the prison and under the supervision of a competent person, assisted by paroled prisoners, a very large bakery, the necessary appliances for which, such as ovens, etc., were brought all the way from Richmond; also a large cook-house, where soup was made and where beans, meat, etc., were cooked, prisoners being detailed for these purposes. They cooked and baked the bread, corn bread, it is true, which could only (unaccustomed as they were to it) of necessity disagree with them; but it was all the Confederate soldiers had, and it was all that could be had. It is well known now that very little wheat was grown in the cotton growing region, the people depending for wheat, flour and bacon on the Western States. It was impossible to feed prisoners on an article which was more than a luxury; it was impossible to get wheat bread even for hospitals. Wheat was a rarity, not only at Andersonville, but everywhere else in the Confederacy. I was sent with official papers on one occasion from the War Department at Richmond to Gen. Lee's headquarters at Orange Courthouse. I arrived at night, about 1 o'clock. The next morning I was asked to breakfast with Gen. Lee and his military family. On the table in front of the General was a little piece of wheat bread, possibly 4 inches long, 2 inches wide and 3 inches thick. The good old gentleman asked each one at the table to have a piece, but all of us knew the scarcity of such food, and each one refused and ate corn bread. If the officers at the Commanding General's table ate corn bread, why not the prisoners at Andersonville? As to the exact weight of each portion of meat or other articles of food issued to the men, I am unable to say; but I am able to say this much of my own personal knowledge: the prisoners got the same rations per man as was issued to the men who did guard duty over them. Could the authorities be expected to give more to the prisoners than to their own men? While on this subject let me add one or two extracts that bear very forcibly on the matter of quantity in the issuing of rations at Andersonville. In an article originally written for the *Southern Magazine*, by Mr. L. M. Parke, of La Grange, Ga., he says:

" I was for three months a clerk in the Commissary Department at Andersonville, and it was my business to weigh out rations for the guards and prisoners alike, and I solemnly assert that the prisoners got ounce for ounce and pound for pound of just the same quality and quantity of food as did the guards.

I find in the Southern Historical Society Papers of March, 1876, a statement from Mr. Jno. F. Frost, a resident of Maine, who had an actual experience of eleven months in Andersonville prison. He says as follows:

"I was orderly of Capt. Folger's Company, 19th Maine; was made prisoner at Petersburg in June, 1864, and was at Andersonville eleven months, or until the war ended. There was suffering among the men who were sick from lack of medicines and delicacies, but all had their rations as fully and regularly as did the Confederate guard. There were times of scarcity, when supply trains were cut off by the Federal forces, and at such times I have known the guard to offer to buy the prisoners rations, being very short themselves. On these occasions the guards would take a portion of their scanty supplies from the people of the country to feed the prisoners. The Rebels were anxious to effect an exchange and get the prisoners off their hands, but it was reported and believed among the prisoners that the Federal authorities refused. At one time I was with a detail of 3,000 prisoners who were marched 200 miles to the coast to be exchanged, but it was declined by the Federal authorities, as was reported, and we marched back with no enviable feelings. I believe that the larger share of the responsibility for the suffering in that prison belonged to our own government. Wirz was harsh and cruel to the prisoners, and deserved hanging; but I believe the Confederate authorities did as well as they could for the prisoners in the matter of clothing, provisions and medicines."

As to the distribution of provisions during my stay at Andersonville, they were hauled in to the Stockade on wagons and distributed, not by Confederates, but by detailed prisoners, several of whom accompanied each wagon. These men could have had no reason to defraud their own comrades. Why should they? The amount was in the wagons for all. The parties had ample opportunity to report any partiality or wrong doing on the part of the distributing agents, and they and the others knew if the reports were well founded the man would be removed, and he knew that his removal from the position of distributor meant at least deprivation of liberties, as well as loss of an extra supply of rations.

I recall now an instance bearing on this subject. Some of the prisoners came to me one morning and said that one of the distributors, Staunton by name, had badly beaten one of the prisoners, because he had attempted either to steal an extra allowance or had terribly abused him (Staunton) about the distribution of provisions. They assured me it was not Staunton's fault, that he had only done his duty; but they also said it would be very unsafe for him (Staunton) to be left inside the prison, as the worst element of the men had threatened to kill him if possible. I was unwilling to act in the matter unadvisedly, or, I should say, without first knowing the whole state of each side of the case, and at the same time I did not care to investigate it myself. At that time the better class of prisoners had arranged a court for trial of such offences; a court similar to the one which in June had tried, convicted and executed six of their comrades for murder and robbery. I therefore told the prisoners they must try Staunton themselves, and if they cleared him I would see he was not injured; while if, after a fair trial, they found him guilty, I would stand by the findings of the court. In order that that the man (Staunton) might not be injured before trial, I took him outside of the prison and kept him under guard until next morning, when he was returned to the custody of the prisoner's court for trial. After a day's sitting the court sent me word that they had fully investigated the trouble and that Staunton had only done his duty. The feeling, however, of the rough element of the prisoners was decidedly against him, and it was asserted that if he was cleared by the court that he would be killed by the prisoners. After his being cleared, the court was afraid to make public their finding, less a riot be brought about, and I was sent for to come to the gate of the prison, and told of the finding of the court, and requested to take Staunton out, as the court and its officers, while they could protect the prisoner for the present, were unwilling to take the risk of keeping the man in the prison after night, and when it should be known that he had been cleared of the charge. This risk was increased, as the man who had been beaten was badly hurt, and his friends were hourly growing more and more clamorous about the matter. I went into the stockade myself, against the advice of my informant, rode to the court tent, and placing Staunton in front of my horse started for the gate. I was forced several times to stop and demand of the surging crowd passage-way for the prisoner. Finally we got to the gate, and Staunton was afterwards kept outside.

As to the sub-distribution of rations, after it left the wagon distributor, I know little. I have been inside the stockade and seen provisions distributed from the wagons, and I have afterwards seen the men dividing their allowance into as many portions as there were men in the squad, and a blind-folded man calling out the names or number of each individual as the head man of the squad pointed to a portion with his finger or a stick. This plan was adopted by the prisoners in order that no partiality could be shown, and to prevent grumbling over an unfair division of rations, and was, I suppose, as good a plan as possibly could be tried under the circumstances.

"In regard to sanitary regulations, there were certain prescribed places and modes for the reception of all filth, and a sluice was made to carry it off; but the most abominable disregard was manifested towards all sanitary regulations, and to such a degree that if a conspiracy had been entered into by a large number of the prisoners to cause the utmost filth and stench, it could not have accomplished a more disgusting result. Beside which there was a large number of atrocious villians, whose outrages in robbing, beating and murdering their fellow prisoners must have been the cause, directly or remotely, of very many deaths, and of an inconceivable amount of suffering."—*New York Day Book*, Jan. 13, 1866.

It has been said by some persons, and will doubtless be said again, that it was the duty of those in charge to make the men obey and attend to the rules and regulations. That may be so under some circumstances, but where you are forced on account of unavoidable reasons to huddle together thirty-four or thirty-five thousand men, with only twelve or fifteen hundred to guard them, you cannot spare men to superintend the cleanliness of each individual. It was for this reason that the prisoners were allowed to organize a police force of their own, establish laws for protection and sanitary benefits; but it seems that they either would not or could not carry out the rules adopted, which were sufficiently good, had they been properly enforced.

I believe that if the greater part of the prisoners had so elected they could have forced those among them who were inclined to disregard cleanliness and health to pay attention to sanitary regulations. It is a well-known fact that when what were known as "the Raiders" were in full force in the stockade, and were day and night murdering and robbing their fellows, then the better men came forward and joined together to put down and punish the marauders; they asked the help of the Confederate authority. In a piece written on Andersonville by a prisoner who was in the stockade a long time, he says: "They granted our request at once, and sent in twenty or thirty of their best men, armed with revolvers, to assist us in hunting out the desperadoes." And again, he says: "Wirz furnished the material for a scaffold and guarded the six unfortunate ones until the appointed day, then delivered them over to us for execution without further assistance on his part."—*Century*, July or Aug., 1890.

At least they were assisted by Capt. Wirz in this matter promptly. Now let me quote from the same writer again:

"A league had been formed by the better class of prisoners. This league, or police, as they were called, was ever after kept up, and constituted itself into a complete government for the stockade." Now, if this league or police "constituted itself a complete government for the stockate," why did they not look after the sanitary condition of the stockade? The filthy condition of it was causing more deaths and suffering among the prisoners than the raiders. The league government would have been sustained and aided in any effort to keep the prison clean as freely and fully as they were aided and sustained in the case of the raiders.

Very much has been said of the cruelty to prisoners at Andersonville. The stocks and chain-gang were punishments used; but I have never heard of a man being tied up by the thumbs—a mode of punishment not only in common use in Federal prisons on Confederate soldiers, but frequently used in United States Army; a punishment the brutality of which is only equalled by the thumb-screws of the inquisition.

As to the promiscuous shooting of men by Wirz himself, or by the sentinels, for the sake of getting

A RECOLLECTION OF THE WAR. 33

furloughs, a charge I have several times seen in print, it is sensational bosh, written and told only to stir up animosity and hate. No furlough was ever issued at Andersonville for such a reason. Such a charge is not worth a thought, nor have I ever heard any one make any specified charge of shooting against Capt. Wirz since his trial. I do remember that during his trial I was confined in the prison at Albany; that I was run off to Fort Warren in order to keep me from being taken, at Wirz request, to Washington to prove that on the specified dates upon which he was charged with murder, which charge was sworn to by three witnesses. I was in charge of the Andersonville prison, and Wirz in Augusta, Ga.

In the *Century* of August, 1890, there appears on page 610 the following:

"The question has often been asked of Andersonville prisioners, did the commander of the prison, Capt. Henry Wirz, ever really murder a prisoner? Yes, and under my own personal observation. On one occasion he rode into the stockade accompanied by two or three attendants also on horseback; the object of his visit was to demand that the Chief of the Union League be delivered up to him, of the crowd that collected about him, not one in fifty knew that such a league existed, and of the actual members of the league few knew who the chief was. Wirz was very soon informed to that effect, which seemed to rouse the demon within him, so that he swore frightfully at the crowd that gathered about him."

"He soon turned to retire from the prison, and while nearly within the gateway drew his heavy revolver and shot the whole six barrels into the crowd of emaciated starving wretches who had collected about him, without stopping to discover the effects of his shooting he put spurs to his horse, sprang out through the gate and galloped away from the stockade. Two men were killed out-right by his shots and several others were wounded."

The date of this alleged shooting is not given, Wirz was not accustomed to be accompanied by mounted attendants, and if on any special occasion he was so attended it was in all probability by officers of Gen. Winder's staff or artillery officers, these would certainly have reported such an action on the part of Wirz or anyone else. I cannot believe any such improbable statement. I never heard of it and I was in a position to know of it, had it occurred while I was at Andersonville or temporarily absent. I have written, however, to Capt. W. S. Winder to ask if he ever heard of such an occurrence, and the following is what he says:

"Such a thing could not have occurred without some of the officers of the guard knowing it, and they never would have been willing to have approved of it by their silence."

Some of the officers of the Florida Artillery would certainly have heard the shooting, and witnessed the excitement, and would never have permitted Wirz to have escaped the punishment he would have deserved.

For such an act to have occurred in such a public place and in such a public manner would have attracted the attention of hundreds of people outside the stockade. I can and do most positively assert that I never heard of that case; and, I do not hesitate to denounce this charge as a most outrageous and wicked one; and I do most positively say, that I never heard of Capt. Wirz shooting any prisoner as was charged on his trial, nor have I ever seen any one who had heard of such shooting. Such a thing could not have occurred without hundreds of people inside and outside the stockade knowing of the fact.

At Andersonville there were more than 1,500 prisoners out on parole in the Quartermaster's, Commissary and Medical Departments, and these men saw and knew everything that was going on at the post. You were in charge of the prison for some weeks, was it possible for you to have shot into the crowd of prisoners at the gate, then dash out on horseback without being seen by the guard at the gate? "I think not." I am convinced Wirz never did this shooting; it looks as if it were like the alleged shooting of one Chicamauga by Wirz, an account of which one Spencer gives in his book. He wrote just after Wirz's trial, and which is based on that trial "An Andersonville Union Prisoner;" says of it in the Brookly *Eagle* of 27th July, '66:

"I was present when this more than miserable man was shot, his own men had been beating him, cripple as he was, they having charged him with giving information to Wirz about a tunnel some of the prisoners had made, but which was discovered. He rushed from them, threw himself under the dead line, demanded of Wirz to be taken outside; Wirz told him to go back and left the platform. "Chicamauga" went off, but again came back and threw himself once more under the dead line. The guard begged the bystanders to take him away; they attempted to do so, but he beat them off with his crutch, and defied the guard to shoot him. The guard did shoot him, but Wirz was not present, and experienced Union soldiers (prisoners) said the guard had no alternative."

There have been many sensational stories told of the cruelty at Andersonville, particularly about Wirz shooting and otherwise maltreating prisoners. But on the trial were two priests, Fathers Whelan and Hamilton, summoned by the prosecution as witnesses against

Wirz. "They were in the stockade day after day for nine months, holding the closest relations to those to whom they were indeed ministering angels, who had opportunities, if any one had, of seeing and hearing everything that took place in and around the stockade, they swore that Capt. Wirz gave them every facility to attend the sick and dying; that he welcomed them to the stockade when they first came there, and they swore they never heard or knew that Wirz shot, or beat, or maltreated a single prisoner at Andersonville."

"On the trial five or six of the most intelligent and respectable men that entered Andersonville gave similar testimony."—*Brooklyn Eagle*, July 27, '66.

I cannot let the subject of Andersonville pass until I have looked at an order, which an article in the *Century* of August, 1890, tells us was issued 27th July, 1864, at Andersonville. It is an order at one time known as "Order No. 13;" then it has been called a circular; which was it, or was it ever issued? Much trouble has been taken to look the matter up, and as I am in possession of pretty good evidence that no such order ever existed, I beg to add here what has been collected on the subject.

The following statement has been furnished me by Capt. W. S. Winder.

The Order, as it appeared in the *Congressional Record* of 22d April, 1890, is as follows:

"Order No. 13."

"Headquarters Military Prison,"
Andersonville, July 27th, 1864.

The officers on duty and in charge of the Florida Artillery, at the time, will, upon receiving notice that the enemy has approached within seven miles

of post, open upon the stockade with grape shot without reference to the situation beyond these lines of defense. JOHN H. WINDER,
Brig.-Gen. Com.

When this order was first published it was denied that any such order had been issued ; but that denial seems to have had no effect, and recently it has appeared in the newspapers, and what is remarkable there seems to be several versions of the same order. The Baltimore *Herald* of September 23d, 1887, contains the following dispatch:

Chicago, Ill., September 22d.

The Federal Ex-prisoners Association is in session in this city.

Gen. Pavey in his address read the following circular issued at Andersonville:

Headquarters
Confederate States Military Prison,
Andersonville, Ga., July 27th, 1864.

The officers on duty and in charge of the Battery of Florida Artillery, at the time, will, upon receiving notice that the enemy have appeared within seven miles of the post, open fire upon the stockade with grape-shot without reference to the situation beyond these lines of defense.

It is better that the last Federal be exterminated than he be permitted to burn and pillage the property of loyal citizens, as they will do if allowed to make their escape from prison.

By order of JOHN H. WINDER,
W. S. WINDER, Brig.-Gen.
Adjt.-Gen.

These orders are supposed to be the same, but they differ very materially. The one which is published in the speech of Mr. Morse is simply an order. The circular as read by Gen. Pavey (it will be seen is not called Order No. 13) gives in addition the reason for issuing it as a part of the order. One had the heading " Headquarters Confederate States Military Prison;" one is signed by Gen. Winder, the other by his Adjutant-General.

When Gen. Winder went to Andersonville, in June, 1864, he continued the use of the order book and letter book, at Headquarters, as used by Col. Person, who had been in command. The last General Order issued, by Col. Person, was No. 44, dated June 14th, 1864. The first General Order issued, by Gen. Winder, was No. 45, dated June 17th, 1864 (this was the order assuming command of the post). The last Special Order issued, by Col. Person, was No. 103, dated June 16th, 1864. The first Special Order issued, by Gen. Winder was 104, dated June 18th, 1864.

It is clearly proven by the above statement that there was no such order as No. 13 issued by Gen. Winder. As for myself, (W. S. Winder) I am prepared to state, under oath, that I never saw, signed or heard of any such order said to have been issued by me as Adjutant General.

Capt. C. E. Dyke who commanded the Florida Artillery, in a letter to me (W. S. Winder) dated Tallahassee, Fla , February 7th, 1876, says:

The order purporting to be No. 13, dated July 27th, 1864; Mr. Blaine recited in his first speech on the Amnesty Bill, directing the officers of my command, upon receiving notice that the enemy have approached within seven miles of the post, to open fire upon the stockade with grape-shot. I have not the remotest recollection of ever having received such an order ; it was inconsistent with Gen. Winder's character.

The following letter is from E. W. Gamble, Esq., a well-known citizen of Tallahassee, Florida, who was a lieutenant in the Battery of Florida Artillery during the time it was stationed at Andersonville:

   Tallahassee, Fla., May 19th, 1890.
W. S. Winder,
 No. 2117 St. Paul street,
  Baltimore, Md.:

Sir—Yours of the 4th, came while I was away from home, calling my attention to the following order purporting to have been given to the Florida Light Artillery then at Andersonville, Ga.

(Mr. Gamble here quotes Order No. 13).

I have to say so, far as I know this is a malicious slander, as no such order was ever given to the Battery, and I feel sure my Captain, Charles E. Dyke, would have made me acquainted of it, as the officers of the company took each a day to be on duty at the guns and it would have been necessary for each of us to have known of such an order.

  * * * * * * * *

   Yours truly,
     E. W. GAMBLE.

Col. F. B. Pavy, now a citizen of Florida, a gentleman well-known and highly esteemed, was first sergeant of the Battery of Florida Artillery while it was stationed at Andersonville, has written the following letter:

   Savannah, Ga., May 12, 1890.
W. S. Winder, Esq.,
 Baltimore, Md.:

My Dear Sir—I am in receipt of your esteemed favor of the 4th inst.; my absence caused delay in replying, which I greatly regret.

I am astonished to learn that your good father was charged with the issuance of the order which you quoted. My relations with Capt. Dyke and the battery he commanded was, perhaps, more close than was ever enjoyed by a soldier occupying my position ; while only a sergeant, I acted and performed more the duties of an adjutant, and was, therefore, in a position to learn even of matters that were confidential. I say to you positively, that I never saw such an order, nor did I ever hear of it.

Yours respectfully,

F. B. PAVY.

Mr. Jackson Marshall who was a clerk in Gen. Winder's office writes as follows :

No. 530 Carey St., Baltimore, Md., November 5th, 1887.

Capt. W. S. Winder :

My Dear Sir—I have received the papers containing the notice of an address delivered by a General Pavy, before the Federal Ex-Prisoners Association at Chicago, at which he read the following order or circular issued at Andersonville :

(Mr. Marshall here quotes the order as given above).

When your father, Gen. John H. Winder, assumed command at Andersonville, June, 1864, I was a clerk at Headquarters and Gen. Winder retained me in that position, giving me charge of all the books in the office. I remained with him till his death, February, 1865.

I have no recollection of having seen or heard of any such order, and no such order was ever entered on the order book by me. It is only another of the many lies that have been circulated in connection with the treatment of the prisoners-of-war. I was almost constantly with Gen. Winder, and knew him to be incapable of anything like inhumanity or inconsistant with true nobleness of character. I resided at Madison, Ga., during the war and at Oxford, Ga., for 15 years before, the home of Secretary Lamar to whom I can refer.

Yours truly,
JACKSON MARSHALL.

Dr. R. R. Stevenson writes as follows:

* * * * * * * *

"As Chief Surgeon of the Andersonville Prison Hospital, I can truthfully say that no such order as that referred to ever emanated from Gen. John H. Winder or his subordinates. I never saw or heard of such an order until after the war, and then it was through a partisan press." * * *

In no instance can I find either in the orders issued by Col. Person or by Gen. Winder, among those in my possession, the heading "Military Prison," or "Confederate States Military Prison." I have examined their general orders down to No. 58 inclusive, and their special orders to No. 114 inclusive. The last general order in my possession issued at Andersonville is No. 58, dated June 30, 1864. The last special order is No. 114, dated July 1, 1864; but the following letter, dated July 28, 1864, the day after the date of the alleged order No. 13, speaks of special order No. 143, which was issued either on the 27th or 28th of July, 1864.

Camp Sumpter,
Andersonville, July 28. 1864.

Captains—

By special order number one hundred and forty-three (143) you will proceed as directed to select a site for a new prison in the neighborhood therein designated. After selecting the site you will secure by rent the land, water privileges, timber and such houses adjacent as may be thought advisable. You will use a sound discretion, conferring with reliable men in the vicinity as to the health of the location, etc., etc. Notify me by telegram as soon as you have made the selection.

Very respectfully,
JOHN H. WINDER.
Brig.-Gen.

Captains D. W. Vowles and W. S. Winder.

When the order read by Gen. Pavy in Chicago was published, I wrote to the Secretary of War asking to be informed if any such order was on file among the Confederate records in his department. He replied as follows:

War Department,
Washington City, Oct. 12, 1887.

Sir—I am in receipt of your letter of the 1st instant requesting a copy of an order said to have been issued by Gen. John H. Winder and dated "Headquarters Confederate States Military Prison, Andersonville, Ga., July 27, 1864," directing the officers in charge of the Florida Artillery, upon receipt of information that the enemy had appeared within seven (7) miles of the post, to open fire upon the stockade with grape-shot.

In reply, I beg to inform you that a careful search has been made, but no record of this order is found on file among the Confederate records.

Very respectfully,
W. C. ENDICOTT,
Secretary of War.

W. S. Winder,
  No. 2117 St. Paul Street,
  Baltimore, Md.

In writing about Andersonville it has been my object simply to state facts. I do not wish for a moment that any one should think I desire to even attempt to say there was no suffering there. I saw it there in its bitterest form; but I do, as I stated in the beginning, wish to lift as far as possible from all connected with Andersonville—from the Confederate government to Gen. Winder, and to the subordinate officers there, the imputation of premeditated cruelty to the prisoners confined there. In further proof of this, I copy from an article in the *Brooklyn Eagle*, July 27, 1866, written by an Andersonville Union prisoner:

"A great meeting was held in the stockade; in fact, every squad of ninety was represented, and after consulting Wirz and Winder, six men were elected to go to Washington to represent the state of the prisoners. Petitions to the Executive were drawn up, setting forth their condition very minutely and accurately. The food, the water, the shelter, and their clothing, the rate of mortality, were all described as they existed, and it might be said the poor fellows went down on the knees of their hearts, asking to be exchanged by their government. These documents were transmitted to Mr. Davis, in Richmond, with the proposition to permit the six delegates to go to Washington. Permission was given. After a few days six of the most intelligent and devoted men among that thirty-five thousand came on as their representatives to Washington."

Now, let me ask if Mr. Davis, Gen. Winder or Capt. Wirz had desired to be cruel and kill out these men as charged, would this permission have been granted? Could they do more to bring about an exchange and release of these men than to send this delegation to plead for themselves? I think not. But what encouragement did the delegates meet with in Washington from their own government? Their own government refused to listen to their prayers and they returned to Andersonville.

Christmas day, 1864, fell on Sunday, consequently the 26th of December of that year was a gala day in the Capital of the Confederacy, as that was the day taken for the Christmas revels.

Who among us who was in Richmond during the four years of the war does not remember the old "Spottswood Hotel." The lobby was full, when about 11 o'clock I went there—full of men, young and old, and they were full of mirth, some full of innocent joy, some doubtless excited by too much of what the Indians call "firewater," the latter class embraced more than its due share of revellers on, that joyous day for the Christmas bowl flowed freely. Richmond was full of officers and soldiers, and the Richmond world was astir.

Threading my way through the crowd, I ran afoul of Harry Brogden, of Maryland, then in the Signal Corps. In course of conversation, he said he had orders to go to Canada with dispatches and that he did not care to go. I had been in Richmond for two or three months, and I was anxious for some change, and seized by sudden impulse, I said I'll go if you do not want to and that remark nearly cost me my life.

In a few hours the orders were transferred and it was arranged that I should leave next morning.

It may be well to say here that the papers I carried consisted of a manifesto from Mr. Jefferson Davis stating that John Beall, of Virginia, was a duly commissioned officer of the Confederate States Navy; that he had been ordered to make the attempt to capture Johnson's island, in Lake Erie, (then used as a prison) and the gunboat Michigan, the particulars of which attempt have been so often published that it is unnecessary for me to repeat here. I also carried a copy of Lieut. Beall's commission as an officer of Confederate States Navy.

If I were to stop now to tell you of how I reached the Potomac river at Mathias' Point and crossed into Maryland, or to give an account of running the blockade, you might well ring the chestnut bell on me, as all those stories are very similar. I shall only say that I crossed the river landing at Pope's creek, Maryland, set out immediately for Washington, saluted the sentinel on guard as I passed over the bridge spanning the Eastern Branch and stood under the shadow of the Capitol—a rebel in Washington.

Nothing of interest happened until the following Sunday, when I reached Toledo, Ohio, where I was detained on account of delayed trains; while sitting in the lobby of the hotel, I think the Oliver House, a United States Naval Officer read from a paper he held in his hands a notice that it had been ascertained that certain papers relative to Beall's case had been sent from Richmond to Canada; that the authorities were on the lookout for the messenger having them in charge. "Ah!" said he, "How I would like to catch the damn rascal who carries those papers; it would be the making of me or any one else that caught him."

The remark was addressed to me, as I sat next to him, and while I very politely concurred in his views "you bet I did not tell him I was the damn rascal." I reached Toronto safely, and after a week started back with my coat sleeves full of closely written white silk and my head full of more important matters committed to memory.

These dispatches were to be taken back to Richmond. The second day out on my return trip, I fell in with a batch of returned Federal prisoners who had been confined at Andersonville, and who had seen me there. This was at a place near Sandusky, at the junction of the Sandusky, Mansfield and Newark railroad with the Toledo and Detroit road. I soon found out I was known, but I could not get off the train; first one then another came and asked me if I was not Davis and if I had not been down South, and although I denied it and produced a pass-port from Canada stating that my name was Cummings, it was no use and when I went to change cars at Newark, Ohio, the Superintendent of the railroad said to a detective this is, we believe, Lieut. Davis from down South; please arrest him, Mr. Brooks. Before being locked up, I was subjected to a diligent search, but Mr. Brooks failed to find the dispatches and I was able to destroy them after I had been put in a cell.

In an article written on the subject the writer says as follows:

"The Provost Marshall, of Newark, was summoned and the prisoner was speedily hurried to the common jail; a search of his person failed to disclose any secret papers, and he was left in the main room with a number of ordinary county criminals. Soon after the military had left the place, the stranger was seen to remove from inside his coat lining a number of dispatches and drawings upon white silk and to burn them in the fire which was blazing in an open stove. The link that would have removed all doubt as to his purposes and condemned him to instantaneous death was thus hopelessly destroyed."

I may state here, however, that the detective, Mr. Brooks, did find my gold watch, assuring me that he could take better care of it than I could, and as he has never returned it, I presume he is caring for it still. The next day I was taken to Columbus, Ohio, and subsequently to Cincinnati for trial; before leaving Columbus, however, I must try, if it is possible, to find language to describe the two nights I spent in the Guardhouse at the *Barracks* in Columbus.

The building in which I was confined, I suppose, was 40 feet long by 16 or 18 feet wide ; I was about to say there were two rooms, but it will be better to say that the room was divided into two parts. The dividing partition being formed of 4x4 scantling, set on end, and so close together as to prevent anything larger than your fist from passing between ; when a man was put in behind this place he was said to be behind the grates, and here the worst class of prisoners were kept, and there I was put. There were 18 or 20 in this pen ; each one ironed, myself included. If I had been kept here any length of time I must have certainly died. I cannot find words to tell you of its filth, nor can I think now of any kind of filth and dirt besprinkled with vermin that I did not see in that room. In all my life, before or since, I have never seen so detestable a place ; no, not at Libby prison or Andersonville.

After some two hours I was taken before the Assistant Provost Marshall. I believe, in fact I am sure, his name was Wilkinson and he was much afraid of being imposed on, and after he had questioned me some time I asked him not to put me in the same place again ; he said, " This fine talking will not do, I must do my duty ;" do it by all means, I replied, but just think a moment, I have not stolen anything or committed any crime to be ashamed of ; I am a soldier and a gentleman, why coop me up with thieves and vagabonds in a pen like that. He thought a moment and then detailed a separate guard to watch me in the other part of the building, not "behind the grates."

When I was taken back to the guardhouse, I was allowed to sit in one corner with a sentinel near me whose special and only duty was to watch me. I was ironed, and of course could not get away, so I had only to sit, and think, and wait developments. In another corner, diagonally from the one in which I was, there was chained to one of the upright posts a soldier, a very large, strong man, crazy from drink, and it seemed the delight of some demons confined in that place to keep him from rest and recovery; if the poor wretch would fall into a doze some passing fiend would kick him and wake him up, in order to hear him swear and rant. Later in the night another demented Italian soldier was brought in and turned loose, he was small, and lithe, and wiry as a cat, he soon saw others teasing the chained man and so followed their example; he would tantalize till the larger man would rush at him, as he glided away while the chain, its limit being reached, would jerk its captive down to the floor with a thud that would have stopped any but a drunken man from repeating the scene. So things went on till morning. Later in the day I was sent to Cincinnati for trial. Arrived at the latter place, I was confined in the third story of a large building known as "McLean Barracks," which was full of prisoners; among them those known as the Chicago Conspirators. I was put in a small room; through a window I could see the other prisoners, but was not allowed to talk to them, and I had to my leg a ball and chain weighing all of 60 pounds; at taps I was ordered to lie down on the floor, I had no bed or blanket and the sentinel was told to shoot me if I raised my head from a block of wood, which was my pillow, before being ordered up in the morning; and so I lived from January 15th till February 1st.

And now came the season of my trial; it only lasted two days, 17th and 18th of January, and was only a form. The evidence was simply to identify me, I plead not guilty to the charge of being a spy. The officer commanding the Department, Gen. Joe Hooker, said, that man is no spy, but the Judge-Advocate General had the findings and sentence approved. The trial began 17th January, 1864; there is little I can say of it now, witnesses who saw me at Andersonville were called to prove my identity, and to swear to my arrest within the Federal lines. I tried to get permission to send to Richmond and to Canada for proof that I was not a spy, simply a bearer of dispatches. I did this to gain time, for it must be remembered up to this time I did not know whether my friends knew of my arrest or no. I have, and I give, the contents below of several printed slips cut from the papers of the time on my application to send to Richmond for evidence. The Judge-Advocate said as follows:

"The Judge-Advocate, Lieut. L. A. Bond, stated to the Court that the accused wished to send to Richmond, Va., to obtain documentary evidence from the Confederate authorities there that he was a bearer of dispatches from Richmond to Canada and from Canada to Richmond, and that he is not now here in the capacity of a spy. The Judge-Advocate remarked: It becomes an important question for the Court to decide whether permission shall be granted, and it might as well be decided at this stage of the proceedings as any other.

I object to any delay in the trial of this case for such a purpose, and my reasons for the objections are: That the so-called Confederate government is not a government recognized by any nation in the world. Those who control the rebel armies are known to us only as traitors in arms in rebellion against the duly constituted and authorized Government of the United States, and any document under the seal of the so-called Confederate States could not be introduced in evidence properly before a military court of the United States. The admission of a document of that kind as evidence would, to a certain extent, be an acknowledgement of the nationality of the insurgent states. They have yet to establish their right to a place among the nations of the earth. Supposing, however, that the accused is permitted to send to Richmond, Va., and obtain from Jefferson Davis or J. P. Benjamin a certificate that he is a Confederate officer, and was the bearer of certain dispatches from Richmond to Canada. Suppose, also, we admit the statement of such certificates to be true; does it necessarily follow that the accused is not a spy? A man may be a bearer of dispatches and also be a spy. The two characters may exist in the same individual. By the laws of war a soldier armed and uniformed may convey dispatches from one army to another, or from a part of an army to another part, and if captured he is entitled to the privileges of a prisoner-of-war; but a soldier who secretely and in disguise enters the lines of the enemy to obtain information and convey it to his own authorities is a spy. The accused in his plea admits that he is a rebel enemy of the United States, and that he entered the lines of the Army of the United States in citizen dress, and that he was the bearer of dispatches from the Rebel authorities at Richmond, Va., to persons in Canada hostile to the United States.

How, then, can it be claimed that the accused should be treated as simply a bearer of dispatches and a prisoner-of-war? When captured the accused was not armed or in uniform, nor was he carrying dispatches to any army or part of an army under the control of the Confederate authorities, unless the Confederate authorities claim to have an army in Canada, a province belonging to Great Britain and presumed to be neutral territory. The accused is a Confederate officer, sworn to uphold the Confederate interest; he is arrested in Ohio, disguised in citizen clothing, attempting to cooperate with certain persons on the soil of a neutral power in acts of hostility towards the United States. Under these circumstances of what avail would be the certificate of Jefferson Davis or J. P. Benjamin, that the accused was a bearer of dispatches as regarded by the laws of war. I therefore submit to the Court whether this case shall be delayed to enable the accused to send to Richmond to procure the certificate he desires."

I always wear a loose collar now, less a tighter one might recall the sensation I experienced when that fellow stopped speaking. It was then it dawned upon me in full force that I was in a tight place, and I could feel in imagination the hempen necktie tighten round my neck, and I might have been strangled to death then and there by fright, if the President of the Court had not asked me if I had anything to say, and I give here the contents of a slip cut from a Cincinnati paper of January 18th or 19th, the time of the trial.

"STATEMENT OF THE ACCUSED.

"'The accused replied that he had little to say in regard to the legal point raised by the Judge-Advocate, but said: that I was a bearer of dispatches I admit freely—wheather a bearer of dispatches is a spy or not my acquaintance with international law does not enable me to say.

"I cannot see why it is that one bearing dispatches through the United States, as rapidly as I can easily prove I did, and in doing which every one must see that I could have no time or intention to make any discoveries to take back to Richmond. I cannot see how such a man can be supposed to be a spy and treated as such.

"I crossed the Potomac on the 28th of December, 1864, having received orders to go to Canada from the Adjutant-General of the War Department at Richmond on the morning of 26th of December. On the 30th I registered as H. B. Stephenson at a hotel in Baltimore, on the same day I took an express train for Detroit, Michigan. Sunday intervening before I had time to reach Canada, I was oblige to lay over at Toledo where you can find me registered in the same name, "H. B. Stevenson," New York," on Monday morning at 3 o'clock I left for Detroit, and at the Russel House there, under date of 2nd day of this year, you may find me registered in the same way; I stayed there long enough only to take breakfast, which can be proven by the proprietors. Immediately after breakfast I crossed the river into Canada, I would not have stopped there at all except to learn whether a passport was required.

"On being informed that none was required to go from here to Canada, although one is required to come from there here, I crossed over to Windsor; there I took the 11 o'clock train for Toronto where I arrived at 9 o'clock the same evening and registed myself in my own proper name S. B. Davis.

"That I was a bearer of dispatches I have nothing to prove save that the prisoners with whom I was confined, on the first night of my arrest, at Newark, saw me take from the inside lining of my under coat my dispatches written on white silk and destroy them.

"The reason I did not admit who I was immediately upon my arrest is, that I knew the witness the moment I saw him and also the other witnesses you have, and I knew that being arrested the way I was would be dangerous.

"My object in denying my name was that I might gain time and opportunity to destroy the dispatches. I was searched, however, and they didn't find them. I can bring the proof that I destroyed the dispatches. My government, if allowed to hear anything of the case, will uphold me simply as a messenger; and the God of Heaven knows it, I have stated the truth.

The court was cleared for the deliberation, the doors were again opened and the Judge-Advocate announced the decision of the court: that the request of the accused was not granted.

The court then adjourned to meet again the following day at 9 o'clock A. M.

When the court met next morning there was little to say or do; the rest was form. I have not a copy of the speech of the Judge-Advocate, but I recollect it was very bitter and he did his best to do his duty as he looked at it, viz: to hang the "Rebel Spy." He said, that "he, (the spy) was brave till captured, but now he asked pity and tried to work on the feelings of the court; but, they, the court, owed a duty to their country and must not allow themselves to be moved by personal feelings of pity or inclination to leniency. He drew a vivid sketch of the rebels burning and plundering along the Canadian frontier, a result this man was trying to accomplish, and closed his address with an assertion that the court could not fail to convict.'"

Again it was my time to say something. I had never made a speech in my life except at school and then I always failed; but I must say something if only to gain time, and I copy now from what the papers printed next day:

"FINAL STATEMENT OF THE ACCUSED.

"Unaccustomed to speak in public to men such as I evidently see this court is composed of, I may well ask you as the school boy in his speech to pass by any imperfections in my remarks.

"Gentlemen—You cannot make me out a spy, when I am convicted simply of carrying dispatches. I can prove they were dipatches by the prisoners with whom I was confined at Newark and by British subjects in Canada.

"They know they contained nothing injurious to the United States Government. There was, so far as I know, nothing in either the dispatches I took or that I was carrying back, that could in the least interfere with the United States or give benefit to the Confederate Government. What I say to you will not have the weight of a feather upon this case, still it is a comfort to one who knows he is innocent to say so to those who hold his life in their hands.

"The dispatches I had did not bear one iota of information as to what was going on within the limits of the United States. What I say may have little weight upon the decision of this court. I hope and believe you are impartial and just men, serving your country as best you may; so I have done, and if it should be my fate to die upon the gallows or by the musketry of an enemy I can look to God with a clear conscience, and look every man in the face that ever breathed, and know that I died innocent of the charge alleged against me. Yes, gentlemen! you may shoot or hang and launch me into eternity before the bar of God, now or whenever it may seem fit; but, gentlemen, that moment the muskets fire or the trap-door falls an innocent man is launched into eternity.

"Gentlemen, I do not ask pity my heart fears nothing on this earth, I am no coward; I, like the rest of you, have faced bullets before to-day. Some of you have marks of them, I can show them, too, I ask not for pity—I ask but for justice. If, in justice, you or any other court of God's globe can make me out a spy, hang me, gentlemen, I am not afraid to die. Young as I am, scarcely verged into manhood, I would like to live; but, gentlemen, I am no coward and I deem one who would stand here before his fellowmen, before soldiers who have faced the foe, who have felt bullets, and ask pity does not deserve the name of man. Had I thought you could have made me out a spy, nothing could have forced me out of Richmond. As to gathering information, I have no way to show that I have not done it; I know I have only done my duty. I have done it as best I could. God knows what I intended and He knows I do not deserve death, but if I die I go without asking pity; but as a soldier should die. I fear not death and I can go to the judgment bar of God now, to-morrow or whenever it may please the Chief Magistrate of this country to say go.

The trial was over. Each member of the Court came and shook hands with me, expressing his personal regret at my unfortunate position, and I was taken back to solitude and my ball and chain. And now came a most trying ordeal, indeed. I had been a prisoner since 11th of January; had been tried for my life and had never had a friendly word or a line from any one on whom I could rely to help me, nor had I any reason to know or think that my friends in Richmond, Canada or Baltimore (where they would be of the most use to me) knew of my position. Can you imagine what the suspense amounted to? Chained, watched by sentinels who had expressed a desire to shoot me, believing my only chance for life was to come from friends with whom I could not communicate, I often wonder how I survived.

After the trial, and when near February 1st, I do not remember the exact date, a gentleman who had known me in earlier days called to see me and said he would notify my friends of my trouble, and that he would do all he could for me, but advised me to prepare for the worse, as he saw no chance for me.

On February 1st, 1865, I found from motions made to me by prisoners whom I could see but not converse with, that something unusual had come to their knowledge about me, and later in the day I saw a slip from one of the daily papers which said I was to be hung February 17th, 1865, and that the sentence had been approved and promulgated by the President of the United States as well as by the Commanding General. That night I was handed the official record of my sentence, which I give in full:

Headquarters Northern Department,
Cincinnati, Ohio, Jan. 26, 1865.

General Order No. 4.

Before a general court-martial which convened at Cincinnati, Ohio, January 17, 1865, pursuant to special orders Nos. 212, 250 and 273, series of 1864, from these headquarters, and of which Lieut.-Col. E. L. Webber, 88th Regiment, Ohio Volunteer infantry, is president, was arraigned and tried

S. B. Davis, alias Willoughby Cummings.

Charge: "Being a Spy."

Specification.—In this, that S. B. Davis, alias Willoughby Cummings, a rebel enemy of the United States, and being an officer in the service of the so-called Confederate States of America, did, on or about the 1st day of January, 1865, secretly and in disguise enter and come within the lines of the regularly authorized and organized military forces of the United States, and within the States of Ohio and Michigan, and did then and there secretly and covertly lurk, in the dress of a citizen,

A RECOLLECTION OF THE WAR. 57

as a spy, and on or about the 12th day of January, 1865, did attempt to leave the said States of Ohio and Michigan, with the purpose and object of going to Richmond, Va., there to deliver dispatches and information from certain parties whose names are unknown, hostile to the Government of the United States, to Jefferson Davis, President of the so-called Confederate States of America, but was arrested as a spy on or about the 14th day of January, 1865, at or near Newark, within the said State of Ohio.

To which the accused pleaded as follows: To the specification, "Guilty," except to the word "lurk" and the phrase "as a spy."

To the charge—Not guilty.

FINDING AND SENTENCE.

The Court, after mature deliberation on the evidence adduced, find the accused as follows:

Of the specification—Guilty.

Of the charge—Guilty.

Two-thirds of the members of the Court concurring therein.

And the Court do therefore sentence him, S. B. Davis, alias Willoughby Cummings, to be hung by the neck until he is dead, at such time and place as the Commanding General may direct.

Two-thirds of the members of the Court concurring therein.

The proceedings, finding and sentence in the foregoing case of S. B. Davis, alias Willoughby Cummings, are approved and confirmed. He will be sent under proper guard by the Commandant of Post, Cincinnati, Ohio, and delivered into the custody of Col. C. W. Hill, Commanding at Johnson's Island, who will see that the sentence in this case is duly executed at that place between the hours of 10 o'clock A. M. and 3 P. M., Friday, the

17th day of February, A. D. 1865, and make due report to the Commanding General.

By command of Major-Gen. Hooker.

         C. H. POTTER,
Official.   Asst. Adjt.-Gen.
 C. H. POTTER,
  Capt. and A. A. G.

On the morning of 2d of February I arrived at Johnson's Island to await the day of execution. I was taken there by Capt. Will Mahon, who was very kind and friendly, and did all he could to make me easy and comfortable. He was very considerate, and on the 1st of February, after he left me, he wrote the following letter:

        Sandusky, Ohio,
        February 1, 1865.

Lieut. S. B. Davis:

Lieut.—I missed the train this afternoon and can't get away before morning. I have just mailed both of your letters and thought probably it would be a satisfaction to you to know it. If there is anything I can do for you, let me know it; you know my address. I felt so glad you were received so kindly at the Island and had so many more privileges than you had before. God bless you!

   Yours truly,
        WILL MAHON.

On the 3d of February I received the first intimation that my friends knew of my trouble and were working for me. It came in the following letter received from the gentleman who had called on me in Cincinnati:

        Cincinnati, Ohio,
        February 2, 1865.

Lieut. S. B. Davis,
 Johnson's Island:

Dear Sir—It may be some consolation to you to

A RECOLLECTION OF THE WAR. 59

know in the sad circumstances in which you are placed that your Baltimore friends are fully apprised of your situation, and will spare no effort to obtain some mitigation of the sentence now resting against you. Still cherish that trust in Providence of which you spoke when I last saw you, and hope for the best while prepared for the worst.

With the same sentiments as heretofore,

I am, etc.,

W. L. M. C.

And now came the struggle to save me. It would be impossible to do justice in words to those kind friends who came forward in that time of great necessity, and I must say here that the hatchet seemed buried for a time in my case, and friends and foes alike aided one another in the common end to be attained. I have several old letters and copies of others which I will insert here, and which lead up to the day of execution.

On the 9th of February there was written a letter by a lawyer to another lawyer in Baltimore, and I desire to make an extract therefrom, as it shows how my case was looked at by the legal fraternity on both sides—I mean Federal, and those who were Southern in their sympathies, for the writer of the letter was a staunch Union man and loyal to the United States:

"I did see General Hooker, in company with Mr. Anderson, on the 20th of January. I stated Davis' case to him. As soon as he heard it he said: '*He's no spy.*' He thanked me for calling his attention to the case and said he would bear my statement in mind when the papers came before him in review. * * * * * *

"You may judge my astonishment on learning the sentence and of its approval by General Hooker. I went to Cincinnati next day, and there learned under a pledge of secrecy (as the condition of the communication), that General Hooker had relied on the opinion of his Judge Advocate, without giving the case his special attention. That the Judge Advocate was satisfied he had erred in recommending the approval of the sentence, and that it was already determined to revoke the order for its execution and to change it to hard labor during the war. I speak of this now because I learn from Colonel Jackson that he has obtained the same information from headquarters and communicated it to you, otherwise I could not mention it.

"I however ignored my information, and on the 2d or February addressed a letter to Burnet, remonstrating against the sentence as a violation, not only of the law, but of the distinction which the human mind involuntarily makes in apportioning punishment according to the magnitude of the offense, and that such extreme punishments must do harm, not only by inviting retaliation but by exciting in the minds of our own people, especially the intelligent and reflecting, a distrust as to the wise and impartial administration of the law by our military tribunals."

The above extract must speak for itself. I think it shows that my plea of not guilty was right, and it was fully proven, if not inside the Court, at least at military headquarters. With nothing to do but think of my rapidly approaching end, my time for the next few days was anything but pleasant. Day after day went slowly, but yet too fast toward the day of execution. On the 8th of February I wrote a letter to the Judge Advocate of the Court which tried me and asked that one or two members of the Court might be present and see me executed. I have before me his original reply which I insert below :

Office Assistant Judge Advocate,
Northern Department,
Cincinnati, Ohio, Feb. 11, 1864.

Lieut. S. B. Davis,
Johnson's Island, Ohio:

Lieut.:—Your communication of the 8th inst. is before me, and I hasten to reply your request that one or two members of the Court which sentenced you to be hung may be present at your execution will be granted if possible. As Judge Advocate of the general court martial which pronounced the sentence of death upon you, I gladly avail myself of this opportunity of saying to you that by your manly conduct and heroic bearing under the most trying circumstances, you have won the respect and excited the admiration of your foeman. A sense of duty to their country alone actuated the members of the Court when they found you guilty of being a spy, and I assure you that so far as I was concerned it was with feelings of regret and sadness that I conducted the prosecution against you. Regret that one so young and brave should deem it right to assist in the destruction of his native land, and sadness that it was my duty to prove him guilty of an offense which merits and receives an ignominious punishment. In that hour of trial may He, who in his mercy tempereth the wind to the shorn lamb, be your protection and support.

Respectfully, etc.,
LEWIS A. BOND,
Lieut. U. S. Volunteers and Asst. Judge Advocate, N. D.

On the 9th there came to me a gentleman whom I had never seen before but who said he was authorized to tell me that I would not be hung. I questioned him closely, but could get nothing further from him; he said I must not let any one on the Island know of this change of sentence; that the commanding officer did not know it, but I could rely on his word. On the 11th I was again told I could rely on his word and by those in authority, but still the officer in charge did not know of any change, and I could get no hopes from him or any one on the Island. This caused me to think I was being deceived and that I was only being held up by false hopes to the end. Hard work was being done, however, to save my life, and I want to insert here several letters and other papers which are of interest only on account of the names signed to them and to show their bearing in the case :

United States Senate Chamber,
Washington, Feb. 8th, 1865.

My Dear Sir—I have only time this morning to write you a line and inclose a rough copy of my proceedings which you will understand. Unwilling to trust even our special messenger, I delivered the original in person this morning.

My impression is that commutation of punishment is certain; but, yet I would relax no effort to obtain full pardon.

All you have to do is to get some political friend of the President to see him. I have done all in power and hope with effect ; I doubted as to the propriety of sending Saulsbury's letter, but several old senators thought differently, so I followed their counsel.   Yours truly,
GEO. REED RIDDLE.
Hon. B. C. PRESSTMAN.

United States Senate Chamber,
Washington, Feb. 7th, 1865.

Sir—Lieut. Sam'l B. Davis, of the Confederate Army, has been sentenced to be shot or hung at or near Cincinnati on the 17th. The object of this letter is a commutation of his punishment, which I respectfully ask. The testimony in the case, to my mind, proves him to be a bearer of dispatches from Canada to Richmond and not "a spy." To all minds there must be a doubt upon the subject, and I trust you will give the prisoner the benefit of the doubt and punish him as a bearer of dispatches ought to be, should you not feel disposed to pardon him in full.

Lieut. Davis was born within a hundred yards of my residence. He is an orphan, being a son of the late Alonzo B. Davis, who was Lieutenant in our Navy and a gallant officer. He is, moreover, the grandson of Col. Sam'l B. Davis, who was the defender of Lewis Delaware during the War of 1812, and has two sisters dependent upon him. The young man is but 20 years of age and has many friends, both in Delaware and Maryland, who would be gratified should you pardon him or commute his punishment.

I have the honor to be,
Respectfully, ect.,
GEO. REED RIDDLE.

His Excellency,
ABRAHAM LINCOLN,
Pres. of the U. S., etc.

I join Mr. Riddle in asking for a commutation of the punishment of death.

[Signed] P. G. VANWINKLE,
" ALEX. RAMSEY,
" N. A. FARWELL,
" IRA HARRIS,
" JAS. DIXON,
" J. C. TEN EYCK.

The subscribers cheerfully unite with Mr. Riddle in his application for the pardon or commutation of the punishment of Lieut. S. B. Davis, of the Confederate Army, convicted as before recited.

[Signed] REVERDY JOHNSON,
" WM. WRIGHT,
" C. R. BUCKALEW,
" T. A. HENDRICKS,
" L. W. POWELL,
" W. A. RICHARDSON,
" EDGAR COWAN,
" GARRETT DAVIS,
" J. W. NESMITH,
" JNO. R. HALE,
" JNO. S. CARLISLE,
" JAS. H. LANE,
" J. B. HENDERSON.

United States Senate Chamber,
Washington, Feb. 7th, 1865.

To the President:

You know I am no political friend of yours. You know I neither ask or expect any personal favor from you or your administration.

Senator Douglas told me, in his life-time, you were a kind hearted man. All I ask of you is to read the defense of this young man, (Sam'l B. Davis) unassisted by counsel; compare it with the celebrated defense of Emmet, and act as the judgment and the heart of the President of the United States should act.

Respectfully, ect.,
[Signed] WM. SAULSBURY.

His Excellency,
ABRAHAM LINCOLN,
President of U. S., etc., etc.

While so much was being done to save my life, there were evidently others doing all they could against me. I never found out who this was until after the war was over and I had been released; but in an extract from a letter which was written August, 1865, when attempts were made for my release from prison, and which I will give in due place hereafter. It seems that Secretary of War (Staunton) and Judge Holt were opposed to me. I copy from a letter written from Cincinnati, February 16th, 1865. "I have heretofore received your telegram in relation to visiting Johnson's island and answered it asking you to 'delay' it, however. The reason of this was my anxiety that no movement should be made in the matter until the 17th (the day fixed for execution had passed) I was the more anxious and indeed sensitive on this point, on account of a very ambiguous telegram which was received here from the President as follows:

"Executive Mansion,
February 13, 1865.

"*Maj. Gen. Hooker:*

"Is it not Lieut. S. B. Davis, convicted as a rebel spy, whose sentence has been commuted; if not, let it not be done. Is there not another person connected with him also in trouble?"

"A. LINCOLN."

"Now a close scrutiny at the wording of this dispatch will at once show that it was the President's intention to have Lieut. S. B. Davis' sentence commuted. It was, however, when first received read as if it was retracting or negativing the order to commute, hence I felt anxious that no further complications should ensue.

"The outside pressure and public comment has been very bitter against him, and quite a storm of indignation will be vented on the head of some one when it leaks out that he has not been hung.

"Under the laws of War and of Nations I felt confident he was not a spy, and hence I have acted in his case.

"I have also been pleased to learn from some Federal officers, who had been prisoners in Andersonville, that Davis treated them with great kindness, and he was actually removed from his position for an act of favoritism to two officers who were visiting, by his consent, a sick comrade."

The 17th was approaching, and on the 15th my attention was called by the guards to the fact that the gallows was being erected and by the night of the 16th it was completed. Still the officer in charge knew nothing of change of sentence, on the night of 16th the guards were doubled at dark and all arrangements made for execution, at 10 o'clock next morning I sent word to the Commanding Officer asking him to dispense with the form of letting me ride to the gallows on my coffin, and told him I could and would walk and give him no unnecessary trouble, and I laid down and slept on the night of 16th of February, thinking honestly that I had seen the sun set for the last time. Finally the 17th came, I rose at 5 o'clock, dressed, ate breakfast and sat down to wait, by 7 o'clock crowds began coming to the Island to see the execution. The band in my hearing was playing the dead march and I saw men stretching some rope which I was told was to be my cravat. I had written a few verses and some of the officers came in to ask for them and my autograph, etc., and things looked desperate. If I may use such and expression, I was mentally dead—all hope was gone. At this time Col. Hill, the Commanding Officer came rapidly to my quarters and sending out all officers and sentinels said : "I have a commutation for you ; your sentence is commuted."

I replied, "I am glad to hear of it sir, to what is it commuted?" To imprisonment during the war. Where? At For Delaware. When do I go? At once. I am ready. The next day the Sandusky papers said: "The commutation was broken to him so gently he showed no feelings." I had no feelings and it was hours before I realized my life was saved.

On leaving the Island I was given a letter from my sister telling me that my sentence had been commuted, and it was dated two weeks before, and had it been given me when received it would have saved me much weary suspense, but it was held till all was over. At Sandusky I past a train load of people going to see me hung, but even to-day I am glad they were disappointed.

On arrival at Fort Delaware I was put into a casemate with several others who were confined there for various reasons. I made up my mind that I would let no opportunity pass me that savored in the least of a chance to escape, and I set to work at once, and in two or three days had made progress enough to be hopeful of success; but my hopes were doomed to disappointment. Some one had been kind enough to inform Secretary Staunton that "if I was permitted to remain in Fort Delaware I would certainly manage to escape and very soon." Consequently, after a week's sojourn there, I was one day taken before General Schoeph, commanding, who informed what was to take place in the following order to a corporal. "You will take this man, put irons on him and take him to Albany; if he attempts to escape, shoot him dead." Turning to me he said: "You hear?" I replied I did, and was soldier enough to understand. After leaving his office I remarked I had handled a very large crowd of Federal prisoners, or had charge of prisons where more prisoners were confined than General Schoeph had ever seen in one body, and I had never ironed a man. This was repeated to General Schoeph and he sent for me and asked what I had said. I repeated ; when with profane and vulgar language I need not repeat here, he ordered his orderly to kick and beat me, while General Schoeph and his adjutant, Captain Ahl, stood by with pistols waiting for a chance to kill me if I resisted in any way. I had gone through too much, however, to be shot for making a useless resistance, feeling assured that no American or brave man would have acted in such a cowardly way.

I was taken to Albany, where I remained until the 1st of September, 1865. I need not recount here the monstrous life I led there. For six weeks I was confined in cell No. 130, then through the kindness of gentlemen in Albany, whose interest had been solicited, I was transferred to the prison hospital, on my promising I would not try to escape. Escape was of no use then, Lee had surrendered and I promised.

All to be done now was to work and hope for release, and everything was done to accomplish it. Once the order was issued, but on its being taken to the War Department, the Secretary destroyed it and said the President had made a mistake.

On the 16th of August, 1865, the following letter was written for the information of those who were working for me :

War Dept., Adjutant-General's office,
Washington, Aug. 16, 1865.

Hon. Reverdy Johnson,
Baltimore, Maryland :

Sir :—In reply to your communication of the 7th inst., addressed to his Excellency, the president of the United States, requesting the remission of the sentence in the case of Samuel Boyer Davis, alias Cummings.

I have respectfully to state that the President declines to interfere with the execution of the sentence as commuted. I remain, sir, very respectfully,
E. D. TOWNSEND,
Assistant Adjutant General.

The following statement is taken from a letter also written in August, 1865:

"When I called, Col. Burnett, Judge Advocate on Gen. Hooker's staff, was in the sitting room.

I asked why Davis was still in prison, as I understood his punishment had been commuted to imprisonment during the war. Burnett said "No, it was imprisonment for life.' 'Is this so.' He also said he had received a severer 'raking down' both from the Secretary of War and Judge Holt for his recommendation in favor of a change of Davis' punishment than for any other of his official acts. That they were both down on him, and that if any steps were taken to procure Davis' release, we ought to avoid Staunton and Holt and go directly to the President."

Of course this showed who my enemies were and no further efforts were made until October, 1865, when I wrote to Gen. Hooker from Fort Warren, where I had been sent September 1st, 1865. In a short time I got the following letter:

Headquarters Department of the East,
New York City, October 25, 1865.

Mr. S. Boyer Davis,
Prisoner-of-War, Fort Warren,
Boston Harbor, Mass.:

Sir—Your letter of the 2d inst. was received during the absence of the Major-General Commanding, since his return I submitted the same to him for instructions.

In reply he directs me to say that the Government has **not** yet declared the war terminated.

That you were transferred from Albany to Fort Warren by order of the authorities at Washington, and in order to gain the information you desire your petition must be addressed to them at Washington. Very respectfully,

Your obediant servant,
WM. H. LAWRENCE,
Brig.-Gen. and A. D. C.

Again headed off, I could only wait developments. October passsed and the dreary days of November were upon us. Worried to death at my prolonged imprisonment I wrote to Mr. P. Bradley, an exchanged prisoner from Andersonville, asking his aid in securing my release. Subsequently I received the following letter from him:

Milford, Mass., November 5th, 1865.

S. B. Davis, Esq.:

Sir—I have been in Washington, on my return I found your note of 28th; am sorry for the delay. In reply, I would say you were the first to introduce any thing like sanitary regulations in the prison at Andersonville; at Savannah, where you had command, the prisoners were treated like men, so far as you were concerned, having plenty to eat —double the amount issued at Andersonville, and of a better quality. You never used any violence and never punished any one for escaping or trying to escape, always telling the prisoners it was their place to get away if they could, and your place, as a Confederate officer, to keep them. All the returned prisoners in this place endorse this.

If I could afford it I would go at once to Washington and state the case to the proper officers.

I intend to call a meeting of our association to be held in January, if you are not released before that time, we will act in the matter. Anything I can do for you, for I believe you deserve it, I am at your command. Write and let me know if you are in want of anything and I will send it.

·Yours truly,

P. BRADLEY,
President Andersonville Prison Survivors Association, Milford, Mass. Box 965.

N. B.—Andersonville Prison Survivors Association : P. Bradley, Milford, Mass., President ; O. B. Fairbanks, Paterson, N. J., Vice-President; Chas. Montgomery, Cleveland, Ohio, Secretary; Jno. M. Lafferty, Phila., Pa., Assistant Secretary; Jas. M. Wright, Fairburg, Ill., Corresponding Secretary.

The dreary days of November were gone, December was upon us. On the 7th of December an officer came to my quarters and handed me the following official order:

War Dept., Adjutant-General's Office,
Washington, Dec. 4, 1865.

Commanding Officer Fort Warren,
Boston Harbor, Mass.:

Sir:—The Secretary of War directs that upon receipt of this order S. Boyer Davis, citizen, and Louis Schermer, late Colonel 15th N. Y. Heavy Artillery, be at once released from confinement and furnished transportation to their homes.

Please acknowledge receipt and report compliance. I am very respectfully,

Your obedient servant,
[Signed,] E. D. TOWNSEND,
Asst. Adjt.-Genl.

Headquarters, Fort Warren, Mass.
December 7, 1865. Official.
[Signed,] LEWIS SMITH,
1st Lt. & R. M. 3d U. S. Art.
Acting Adjutant.

On my arrival in Baltimore I saw a gentleman who had that day come from Washington, and who came to notify my friends that it was impossible to have me released, as Staunton was very bitter and said I "ought to have been hung." He could not understand how I got out of prison, and Staunton afterwards said it was a mistake.

I am very sure that many having read this little story of the war have thought often during its perusal, "I wonder how that fellow felt when they were about to hang him?"

Now, I cannot tell you, nor do I believe that any one under similar circumstances can tell you. I once heard a darky preacher describe hell, or tell what he knew about it. He said: "I don't know if there is such a place, I don't know if there is fire there or sorrow there or if there is anything there, but, brothers and sisters, I don't want to go there if it is nothing but smoke."

And I don't want to feel as I did from 1st to 17th of February, 1865, again, even if it ends as it did then, only in smoke.

www.ingramcontent.com/pod-product-compliance
Lightning Source LLC
Chambersburg PA
CBHW020239090426
42735CB00010B/1767